| DATE DUE | | | |
|---|---|---|---|
| | | | |
| | | | |
| | | | |
| | | | |
| | | | |
| | | | |
| | | | |
| | | | |
| | | | |
| | | | |
| | | | |
| | | | |
| | | | |
| | | | |

**591.9**
**MUZ**

Muzik, Katy.

At home in the coral reef.

# At Home
## in the
# CORAL REEF

by Katy Muzik
Illustrated by Katherine Brown-Wing

## Charlesbridge

To the Water. *K.M.*
For Susan D. Gibbs and my husband Stephen. *K.B.W.*

Text and illustrations Copyright © 1992 by Charlesbridge Publishing
Library of Congress Catalog Card Number 92-70577
ISBN 0-88106-487-4
Published by Charlesbridge Publishing, 85 Main Street, Watertown, MA 02172 • (617) 926-0329
Printed in the United States of America
10 9 8 7 6 5 4 3 2 1

Down down down down in the tropical clear blue sea lives a beautiful coral reef.

The coral reef is a wonderful home for hundreds of kinds of fish and thousands of other kinds of creatures.

The reef itself is made of zillions of tiny animals called coral polyps.

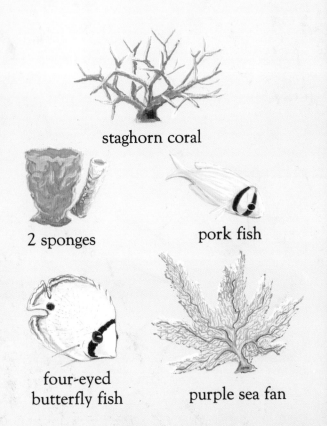

staghorn coral

2 sponges

pork fish

four-eyed butterfly fish

purple sea fan

Each tiny coral polyp catches food with its little arms, called tentacles. The polyps share their food and live so close together that their skeletons are connected.

Some kinds of coral polyps make soft skeletons that sway gently back and forth in the water. These polyps have 8 tentacles.

Other coral polyps make skeletons that are as hard as rock. Their hard skeletons form the coral reef. A hard coral polyp has 12, or 24, or 48, or more tentacles!

Together, over 50 kinds of hard coral form this reef in the Caribbean Sea.

neon goby

spotted drum

4 staghorn
coral polyps
(hard coral)

sea whip coral
(soft coral)

What are these pink things?

Coral eggs! Once a year, coral polyps have babies. Eggs and sperm pop out of the polyps and float up and up and up to the top of the blue sea. There each fertilized egg becomes a baby coral called a planula. Now it is ready to search for a new home.

The planula is completely covered with little hairs. It swims by waving them through the water, but it cannot swim very fast.

Watch out, little planula! Watch out for those hungry wrasses!

Whoosh! Just in time, a big wave carries the planula away to . . .

coral egg          planula

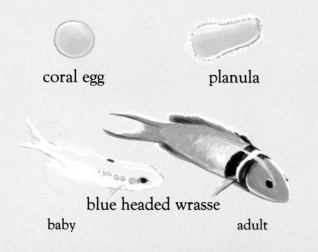

blue headed wrasse

baby                    adult

the crest, or top, of the coral reef.

Here the water is very shallow. Because it is so shallow, the waves break and crash into the reef.

Splash! Crash! The breaking waves make the water very rough. It's so rough that only a few animals can live here. A fireworm holds on tight. A school of blue tangs darts in and out, hunting for food.

Crash! Splash! Will this be home for the planula? No, it's too rough. The planula is swept along, riding a wave over the crest to . . .

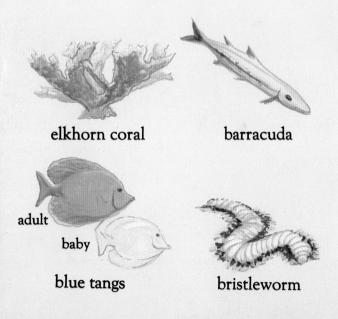

elkhorn coral

barracuda

adult

baby

blue tangs

bristleworm

the lagoon.

The water in the lagoon is calm. Although the lagoon seems peaceful, it is really a busy place, from top

to

bottom.

At the top, a pelican gulps a pouchful of fish. At the bottom, a stingray slurps up shrimp.

Many animals looking for food in the lagoon are hard to see. An emerald clingfish hides on a blade of turtle grass. Clams and crabs hide in the sand.

Such a busy place, day and . . .

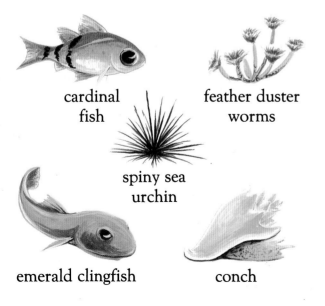

cardinal
fish

feather duster
worms

spiny sea
urchin

emerald clingfish

conch

night in the lagoon.

Flash! Glow! Blink! What could these lights be? They twinkle like stars in the sky, but they are all under water!

These lights are made by animals. Animals almost too small to see are twinkling. Brittle stars flash to scare away lobsters and crabs. Worms glow to show other worms where they are. Flashlight fish attract their food by blinking.

Can the planula live here? No, it is too sandy. The planula needs a rocky place. It floats along to . . .

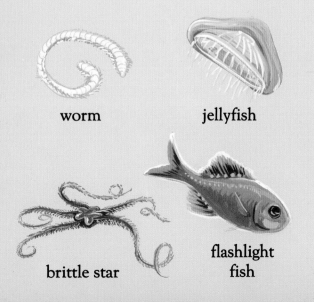

worm

jellyfish

brittle star

flashlight fish

the red mangrove trees near the shore of the lagoon.

Red mangroves can grow in salty water. Their roots grow out and hang down right into the ocean. Sponges and seaweeds grow on the roots.

Millions of baby fish and baby shrimp start life in the water around mangrove roots. There's lots of food for them there.

Will this be a home for the planula, too? No, the water here is too shady for the planula. It turns away and swims along to . . .

mangrove tree

oysters

baby grunt

mangrove crab

the shallow water near the beach of the lagoon.

The sunshine heats the sandy beach. The sand was made by the ocean waves. Over thousands of years, the waves have pounded the skeletons of reef animals and plants into smaller and smaller bits. Eventually, the bits formed so many grains of sand that they covered the bottom of the lagoon and washed up on shore to make a beach.

Will this be home for the planula? No, it's too shallow and too hot here. The planula catches a current to . . .

sea urchin and spine

halimeda plant

bits of sand

flaming tongue snail

staghorn coral skeleton

deeper water. Oh no, the water is dirty!

The water is so dirty, the coral is dying. The dirt smothers the coral polyps and blocks the sunlight they need.

Chemicals washed down the rivers from factories and farms poison the coral. In the dirty water harmful bacteria grow over the coral and kill it. Careless divers hurt the coral too. They step on it and break it with their boat anchors.

Without living coral, the fish and other animals will leave. The planula cannot live here either. Luckily, a current carries it out of the lagoon, over the top of the reef, and down . . .

Nassau grouper

black band bacteria on brain coral

slimy bacteria

the other side of the reef
deeper
and deeper
and deeper
to a healthy part of the reef.

At last! A safe spot for the planula to settle down. The spot is hard and rocky. It's sunny but not too hot. Gentle currents bring clean water, and plenty of food.

It will be a perfect home!

manta ray

squid

close-up of a
star coral polyp hiding

Christmas tree
worm

Surprise! The planula is changing. First, it sticks itself to a safe spot. Then, around its mouth it grows twelve little tentacles. Now it is a polyp. It looks like a flower, but it really is an animal.

Under its soft body, the polyp starts to grow a hard white skeleton. In a few weeks it makes another tiny polyp exactly like itself. The polyps are connected to each other. Together, the two polyps have twenty-four tentacles for catching food.

Oh, a little copepod! Catch it!

copepod

1 month    6 months     1 year

a planula grows up

The planula is growing up to be a staghorn coral. More polyps grow, and more and more.

Here comes a reef butterfly fish. It eats coral. Quick, tiny polyps, hide!

The coral polyps warn each other of danger. Quick as a wink, they hug their tentacles in. They hide their soft bodies down inside their hard white skeleton.

When the danger is past, the coral polyps slowly come out and open up their tentacles again.

staghorn coral
2 years old

feather star

giant sea fan

sea squirts

Many creatures in the reef are partners that help each other hide or find food. A crab hides in the coral to escape from a hungry octopus. A shrimp lives safely inside a vase sponge.

At a cleaning station, gobies eat what they clean from the teeth of a big grouper. The grouper holds its mouth wide open for the gobies. Away from the station, the grouper would eat gobies!

Even the tiny polyps have partners. The polyps get special food from little golden plants living just inside their skin. In return, the plants get a home. This partnership helps the coral grow big enough to form reefs.

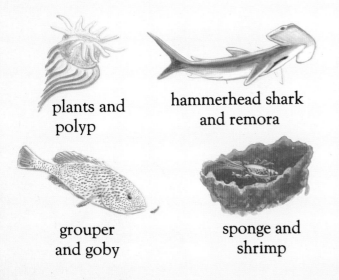

plants and polyp

hammerhead shark and remora

grouper and goby

sponge and shrimp

Do<sub>w</sub><sub>n</sub> d<sub>o</sub><sub>w</sub>n d<sub>o</sub><sub>w</sub><sub>n</sub> in the tropical clear blue sea, this coral reef is alive and well. The place where it lives is clean. Zillions of coral animals have been adding their skeletons to the reef for over 8,000 years.

It takes thousands of years for a reef to grow but only a few years for one to be destroyed! This reef and other coral reefs all around the world are in danger because the oceans are becoming dirty. Coral reefs need our help.

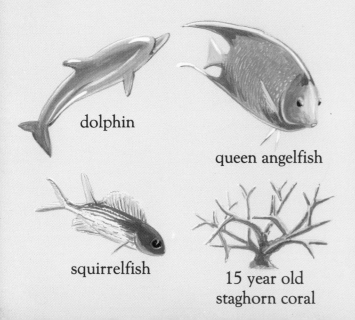

dolphin

queen angelfish

squirrelfish

15 year old
staghorn coral

What can we do to help a little baby planula grow up to become part of a big coral reef? The first step is to discover how what we do on land affects life in the sea.

All living creatures — including corals and people — need clean water. We all use water on our farms, in our suburbs, and in our cities. We throw many things into it that make it dirty. This dirty water flows into rivers, lakes, and underground streams, and eventually ends up in the sea. There it hurts the coral reef and all the creatures that make it their home.

But we can make a difference. We can make our rivers and lakes and oceans clean again. We can learn about life on the coral reef and share what we learn. We can help people everywhere to care about the amazing reefs and the tiny coral animals that build them.

## DUNES

Wave-like sand formations that are created by wind. Most sand dunes are located near the sea or in a desert.

## RIDGE

A string of hills or mountains that form a continuous elevated range. The peaks of a ridge often have their own names. Altogether, the silhouette created by these mountains and hills is called the ridgeline.

## GULCH

A narrow ravine with steep sides surrounding a fast-moving stream.

## GLACIER

A large mass of ice that moves very slowly, spreading out on a land surface. Glaciers leave behind valleys and unusual land formations.

## ISTHMUS

A long, narrow strip of land that connects two bigger land masses that are separated by water.

## TAIGA

A swampy forest usually found in the northern parts of the globe, between tundras and steppes. The taiga is home to billions of trees and makes up one of the world's largest biomes.

## ALPINE LAKE

A lake or reservoir high above sea level and surrounded by mountains. Alpine lakes tend to be very clear because of the cold mountain water that empties into them.

## CHAPARRAL

A group of shrubby bushes that are fit for dry summers and moist winters. Chaparrals are home to many animals, like jackrabbits, coyotes, mule deer, and alligator lizards.

## FOOTHILLS

A range of small hills at the foot of a mountain. Many mammals live on foothills, like mountain lions, bobcats, coyotes, and skunks.

## VISTA

A view that is usually dramatic in scope. Often a vista is an established viewing spot from atop a mountain, ridge, or mesa.

## BADLANDS

A region with limited vegetation and uniquely formed, rough hills. Badlands are mostly found in the United States in southwestern South Dakota and northwestern Nebraska.

## TUNDRA

A flat area without trees that consists mostly of mosses, lichens, herbs, and dwarf shrubs. Tundras exist in frozen subsoil parts of North America, Asia, Europe, and the Arctic.

## FJORD

A long, narrow inlet of the sea in between frozen, icy cliffs. Norway is known for its beautiful and plentiful fjords.

## ATOLL

A circle-shaped coral reef or group of islands that surrounds a lagoon. Atolls are formed by underwater volcanoes.

## ARCHIPELAGO

A group of islands. Usually these islands are relatively close together, like pebbles thrown into the sea.

## ESTUARY

An area where a river or stream carrying fresh water meets the saltwater ocean. Many fish, birds, crabs, and other creatures live in or near estuaries.

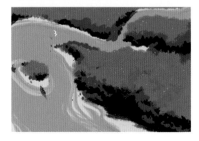

## OASIS

A green, moist area in the middle of the desert. Water is found in an oasis, so it's sometimes called a watering hole. A thirsty traveler in the desert always hopes for an oasis.

## LAGOON

A large area of calm sea water. Lagoons are always close to or lead to bigger bodies of water, like oceans or bays, but are separated from them by things like barrier islands, low sandbanks, or coral reefs. A lot of times, people like to kayak or canoe on lagoons.

# Glossary

### STEPPE

A wide plain usually covered with grass or other low growth. Steppes are found in places where there are hot, dry summers and short, rainy winters.

### GORGE

A narrow valley in between steep rock formations or mountains. Gorges are often dramatic in their appearance, and at the bottom there is often a river or stream.

### VALLEY

A low range of land separating mountains or hills. Valleys often have a river flowing through.

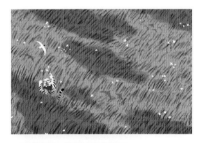

### PLAIN

A flat piece of land with very few trees. Plains are often turned into farmland. The midwestern United States is largely plains.

### CLOUD FOREST

A moist, always-green forest constantly covered by clouds or fog. Most cloud forests are in Central America, but they can also be found in South America, Africa, Southeast Asia, and the Caribbean.

ISTHMUS

GLACIER

GULCH

# DUNES

FOOTHILLS

CHAPARRAL

ALPINE LAKE

LAGOON

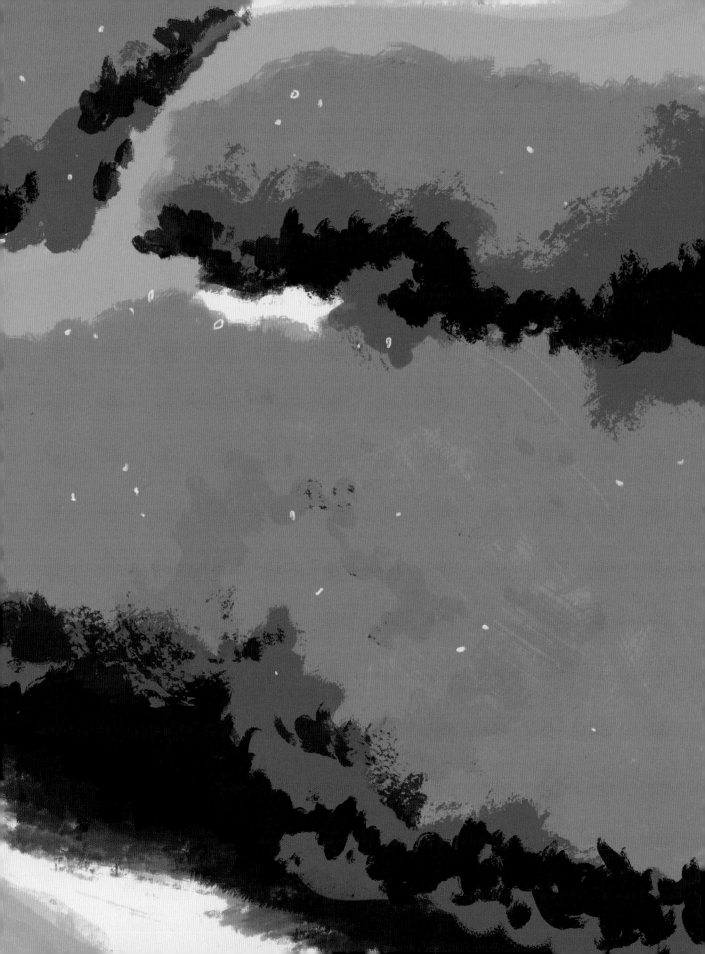

ESTUARY

# ARCHIPELAGO

ATOLL

FJORD

CLOUD
FOREST